Al
O

MW01076243

CAUTION: Professionals and amateurs are hereby warned that this play is subject to royalty. It is fully protected by Original Works Publishing, and the copyright laws of the United States. All rights, including professional, amateur, motion pictures, recitation, lecturing, public reading, radio broadcasting, television, and the rights of translation into foreign languages are strictly reserved.

The performance rights to this play are controlled by Original Works Publishing and royalty arrangements and licenses must be secured well in advance of presentation. PLEASE NOTE that amateur royalty fees are set upon application in accordance with your producing circumstances. When applying for a royalty quotation and license please give us the number of performances intended, dates of production, your seating capacity and admission fee. Royalties are payable with negotiation from Original Works Publishing.

Royalty of the required amount must be paid whether the play is presented for charity or gain and whether or not admission is charged. Particular emphasis is laid on the question of amateur or professional readings, permission and terms for which must be secured from Original Works Publishing through direct contact.

Copying from this book in whole or in part is strictly forbidden by law, and the right of performance is not transferable.

Whenever the play is produced the following notice must appear on all programs, printing, and advertising for the play:

"Produced by special arrangement with
Original Works Publishing.
www.originalworksonline.com"

Due authorship credit must be given on all programs, printing and advertising for the play.

Paper Cranes
© Kari Bentley-Quinn
Trade Edition, 2014
ISBN 978-1-63092-035-7

About the cover

Mariëlle Coppes committed to making 1000 paper cranes and handed them out to 1000 strangers as part of her series of "Magical Daydream" feel-good projects designed to brighten people's day.

You can follow her paper crane journey on her blog here:
http://www.magicaldaydream.com/2013/07/1000-cranes-for-1000-strangers.html

Enjoy the video result of Mariëlle's journey here:
http://youtu.be/VgD22_rLw7E

Paper Cranes

A play by Kari Bentley-Quinn

Setting: A suburb

Time: The present, mid summer to mid fall

Cast of Characters:

MONA (F, young looking 40's)
DAVID (M, mid 30's)
MADDIE (F, 19)
JULIE (F, early 30's)
AMY (F, early 30's)

The World Premiere of PAPER CRANES was produced by Packawallop Productions and directed by Scott Ebersold. It opened on April 15, 2011 at The Access Theater in New York City. The original cast and crew were as follows:

CAST (In order of appearance)

MONA:	Cynthia Silver
AMY:	Susan Louise O'Connor
DAVID:	Eric T. Miller
JULIE:	Melissa Hammans
MADDIE:	Sarah Lord

CREATIVE TEAM

Director:	Scott Ebersold
Assistant Director:	Kyle Fox
Production Stage Manager:	Amy Francis Schott
Stage Manager:	Justin Boudreau
Properties Manager:	Danielle Schultz
Set Design:	Jared Rutherford
Costume Design:	Jennifer Paar
Lighting Design:	Scott Bolman
Sound Design:	Ryan Maeker
Assistant Sound Design:	Chantel Pascente
Publicity:	Lanie Zipoy
Casting:	Judy Bowman Casting

Paper Cranes

ACT ONE

Prologue

(MONA is seated by a small desk in a small room, where hundreds of origami paper cranes hang by dental floss from the ceiling, stacked on top of one another. They are plentiful and overwhelming. Mona is forty-two years old, well dressed, elegant. Her grief hangs over her like a thick fog.)

MONA: There's a letter in the top drawer of our desk.
It is neatly folded into a neat little envelope, embossed with our initials.
The stationery was one of the first nice things I bought before our wedding.
I bought it to write thank you notes on.
Do you remember where I found it?
That amazing little place in the Village on our trip to New York?
That's where I saw the paper, perfectly square, clean right angles.
Cream colored linen with Wedgwood blue borders, woven together and sturdy, like we were.
It was perfect.

When I was a little girl,
I'd read a book about a little girl named Sadako who lived in Hiroshima.
She survived the atomic bomb, but got leukemia from the radiation years later.
When she found out she was sick, she began to fold paper cranes.

It is thought that anyone who folds 1000 cranes will be granted a wish.
Her wish was to live.

When you started slipping away, I remembered Sadako and her birds.
I went to the art store and bought packages and packages of paper.
I sat by your bedside and folded them for you.
I folded what seemed like millions, but I didn't fold enough, I guess.
I wish you could have seen them.

All I have left of you now is your letter.
It's still in the top drawer of our desk
I still haven't opened it.
I don't know if I ever will.

For now I keep on folding and unfolding
As if the cranes will somehow take flight
As if they'll save you this time.

(AMY and DAVID are both in spotlight)

AMY: I couldn't tell you why I do it.
There are junkies, desperate and frothing on street corners
Then there's me.
I guess there's really no difference.
I've grown weary of the setup,
Meeting in a public place, making awkward small talk
Deciding on the various implements, preferred brand of latex, lube
When what we both want and need is just a moment away.

I'm not looking for safety, I'm looking for the sick rush of anticipation
The moment when I must give in, and then, then I am not me
I am Lady Godiva on horseback, head thrown back, hair aflame
I am the beautiful ingénue in a vampire film
I am in spygear, leather and latex
I know it's dangerous.
And yet, I need what they give me
I need to submit and they need to control
I need to change to stay the same.

DAVID: I couldn't tell you why I do it
It's never the same, and I always expect it to be
I set it all up, I go through the steps
I see what have become countless, faceless asses
Upturned, red handprints on white flesh
And I should feel what I felt then
And yet I am unmoved, unloved
A heroin addict placated with methadone
Empty substitutes for her, whose hands I'd kiss at dinner
Across the table, still sweet with perfume
Whose hands I bound with satin ties to the bedpost
The same hands that were thrown around my neck when I untied her,
Cradled her, kissed her in extremities of gratitude and love
I thought I'd never see such things again
Until, one night, late, I received a picture.

AMY: I sent him my picture, and his response was exciting
I asked him what he wanted, what he liked
And his response was "I only request your silence".

DAVID: I opened her picture
I don't ever want to hear the sound I must have made
I don't want to think about it.
Oh god, I am a leech, I know this, a bottom feeder
A pestilence, and yet
There she was, an unanswered prayer.

AMY: My instructions were simple
I was to wear all black – undergarments, dress, shoes
And I wasn't to speak once it began
Not a word.
If I had to moan or cry out, I had to find a way to
muffle it or I'd be gagged
"What, you don't like it when a girl moans?" I asked,
playful
He didn't answer that.

DAVID: I promised I wouldn't hurt her.

AMY: I said I wanted him to hurt me.

DAVID: I meant it.

AMY: He said he wouldn't have to.

DAVID: I didn't know what I meant.

AMY: I was turned on.
What could he mean?

DAVID: I'm still not sure what I meant.

AMY: 8 o'clock, he said.
Don't be late, or else.
I turned the computer off, ran upstairs and made my-
self come

Twice, panting, screaming
And thinking, spent, in the dark
What's wrong with me?

DAVID: Alone, later, in the dark
I stared at the ceiling, and I thought
What's wrong with me?
What the fuck is wrong with me?

Scene 1

(Amy is standing outside of a loud bar. JULIE enters, fanning herself, sweaty. The music can be heard pounding in the background. MADDIE is by herself on the other side of the stage, drinking a beer. Maddie is young and what could best be described as very soft butch. Julie leans into Amy.)

JULIE: So hot in there...

AMY: You want another drink?

JULIE: I dunno. I'm pretty hammered.

AMY: Wanna beer?

JULIE: Yes! Beer!

AMY: Not vodka.

JULIE: No more vodka!

AMY: Just say no!

JULIE: No! Beer please!

AMY: Okay, drunkie. I'll be back.

(Amy exits. Julie walks out to where Maddie is standing. She fans herself.)

MADDIE: Hot in there, right?

JULIE: I'm sorry?

MADDIE: It's hot. Inside.

JULIE: Yeah...

MADDIE: I think they do it deliberately to make you drunker.

JULIE: I'm pretty drunk.

MADDIE: Are you?

JULIE: Hell yeah. $3 vodka tonics? In July? Not good.

(Julie closes her eyes for a moment, scoops her hair up. Maddie is staring)

JULIE: What about you?

MADDIE: I could be drunker, honestly. My friend completely ditched me. She left with this girl...she was cute, but worth ditching me for? I think not.

(Maddie pulls out a pack of cigarettes)

MADDIE: Want one?

JULIE: Oh, I don't...
(Changes her mind)
    ...yes. Yes, I would. Thank you.
(Maddie hands her a cigarette, lights it for Julie, lights her own)
    I'm Julie.

(Julie holds out her hand. Maddie takes it, flirtatiously)

MADDIE: Madison. But call me Maddie.

JULIE: Madison. Like the avenue?

MADDIE: Like millions of other white girls my age.

JULIE: Are you even old enough to be here?

MADDIE: You here with anyone?

JULIE: Oh…yeah…Amy. She's just a friend though… not like you need to know she's a friend, cause you didn't ask, but…well, I guess she's sort of my ex-girlfriend, even though she's not even GAY, really…

MADDIE: If she's not gay, why is she at a dyke bar?

JULIE: I'd better go find her.

MADDIE: Am I making you nervous?

JULIE: What? No.

MADDIE: It seems like you're trying to get away. Do you think I'm ugly or something?

JULIE: Of course not.

MADDIE: You think I'm cute, then.

JULIE: In the way teenagers are cute. The dangerous, illegal way.

MADDIE: I'm nineteen. That's not illegal.

JULIE: It probably should be.

MADDIE: You're beautiful, you know.

JULIE: I bet you say that to all the girls.

MADDIE: Maybe.

(Beat)

JULIE: So what do you do for fun besides chase old ladies at gay bars?

MADDIE: I'm in school.

JULIE: Where? The university?

MADDIE: No. Not right now. Community college. Just for a year, or two...not really sure what I want to be when I grow up.

JULIE: You're never going to know what you want to be when you grow up.

MADDIE: That's what everyone tells me.

JULIE: You're probably smart. I'm an indentured servant to my student loan company.

MADDIE: What was your major?

JULIE: Sculpture.

MADDIE: Practical!

JULIE: Very!

MADDIE: So you're an artist?

JULIE: No. I'm a paralegal.

MADDIE: I won't hold it against you. You're sexy anyway.

JULIE: You think so, huh?

(Maddie leans in and kisses Julie softly, almost innocently. Her hands trace the small of Julie's back. Maddie smiles at her)

MADDIE: Wanna go somewhere quiet?

JULIE: I can't…my friend is--

MADDIE: Your friend is what?

JULIE: Coming back.

MADDIE: She's not here yet, now is she?

(Maddie pushes her up against the wall and kisses her again, not innocently this time. Amy enters, carrying two beers. Amy watches them for a moment, intrigued, and then clears her throat. Julie breaks the kiss off.)

JULIE: Hey…hi! Hey…oh, you got beer, fantastic…

(Amy hands a beer to Julie, who begins drinking it quickly)

AMY: Yes, finally. It's a mob scene in there…good to see you've been, ah, making friends…

JULIE: Oh, right…Maddie, this is my friend Amy. Amy, this is Maddie…Maddie is, uh—

AMY: Enchanté.

(Amy takes the cigarette from Julie, takes a drag, hands it back to Julie)

MADDIE: Nice to meet you.

JULIE: So, uh, yeah we were just talking about—

MADDIE: Sculpture.

JULIE: Yes. Sculpture.

AMY: I see.

MADDIE: I gotta pee. I'll be right back...you still gonna be here?

JULIE: Yeah. Yeah, I'll be here.

(Maddie exits. Amy and Julie crack up)

AMY: The last thing I expected to see when I came back was you getting felt up by a sixteen year old.

JULIE: She's nineteen. Or so she claims...

AMY: At least she's legal.

JULIE: Listen...we better go, right? This is a bad idea. This girl is trouble.

AMY: With a capital T. All the more reason for you to take her home.

JULIE: Oh come on!

AMY: You want to sleep with her. I can tell. I don't blame you, she's cute.

16

JULIE: You're just doing this so you can hold it against me.

AMY: Not true! Get down girl, what do I care? Besides, I'm hammered. I should get home.

JULIE: Please take a cab.

AMY: What did you think I was gonna do, walk? You're the one who drove here.

JULIE: Did I? Shit.

AMY: Don't drive.

JULIE: I won't.

AMY: Good.

JULIE: Don't leave me. This is bad decision making. Very bad.

AMY: I'll call you tomorrow.

(Amy downs the rest of her beer and exits. Julie waits alone for a moment, fighting with herself silently, until Maddie re-appears.)

MADDIE: You waited.

JULIE: I waited.

MADDIE: You got a car?

JULIE: I probably shouldn't drive.

MADDIE: I can drive. I'm not drunk.

JULIE: Where are we going?

MADDIE: Your place?

JULIE: I thought you wanted to go someplace quiet.

MADDIE: Is your place not quiet? Besides...I got a...
uh...roommate. Uptight.

(Julie takes her keys out of her pocket and hands them to Maddie.)

JULIE: All right. You win.

MADDIE: I always do. But that's a good thing. You'll
see.

(Maddie walks off, flirtatiously. Julie follows.)

Scene 2

(It is early morning. Maddie tiptoes into her house. Mona is seated at her desk with the cranes.)

MADDIE: Mama? Hello?

MONA: In here!

(Maddie stands at the door but does not enter. Mona is writing. At her feet are countless crumpled pieces of paper.)

MADDIE: Whatcha doin'?

MONA: Working.
(Beat)
    Out all night?

MADDIE: Yeah. Crashed at Nellie's house.

MONA: You most certainly did not crash at Nellie's house because I ran into her at the convenience store. At 1 am.

MADDIE: Why were you at the convenience store at 1 am?

MONA: Couldn't sleep.

MADDIE: Again?

MONA: Make sure you always have a condom with you.

MADDIE: You don't have to worry about that, Mama.

MONA: Next time, just text me something like "Not coming home tonight, not dead in a gutter…"

MADDIE: Next time. I promise.
(Beat)
You look exhausted. You should take an Ambien tonight.

MONA: I don't have Ambien.

MADDIE: I do.

MONA: Where'd you get them?

MADDIE: Dr. Casey.

MONA: She shouldn't be giving sleeping pills to a 19 year old.

MADDIE: They helped me sleep for finals. Don't need them anymore.

(Maddie takes the pill bottle from her purse, hands it to Mona)

MONA: Thanks.
(Mona takes a package of origami paper from her drawer, shows it to Maddie)
Look what Sheila brought me from Tokyo.

MADDIE: More paper.

MONA: Yes. It's the perfect size and weight. Clean, crisp folds. Perfection.

MADDIE: Aren't you running out of room in there?

MONA: I'm folding a thousand for the Children's Hospital.

MADDIE: You're gonna give yourself carpal tunnel.

MONA: It focuses me.

MADDIE: I think I'm gonna lay down for a little while.

MONA: Okay.

MADDIE: Maybe we should get dinner tonight? Just us girls.

MONA: I've got work to do. These deadlines aren't meeting themselves.

MADDIE: Oh. Okay.

MONA: Next week. Promise.
(Maddie begins to exit)
Sleep tight, cherie.

MADDIE: Bonne nuit, Mama.

(Maddie exits. The lights come back up on Mona's room. On the other side of the stage is David's bedroom. Amy's purse is on the floor near the bed.)

DAVID: Five minutes
All I need is five minutes to hold you again, to feel the warm softness of you
To twirl a strand of your hair between my fingers.
She's an almost perfect replica.
Missing the birthmark
But almost exact.

(Amy enters)

DAVID: Are you ready?

AMY: Yeah. I'm ready.

(David stands behind Amy.)

DAVID: Undress.

(Amy starts with shoes - David stops her from removing them. Amy slides her black dress off. She is in very expensive and carefully purchased black lingerie – bra, panties, garters. The expensive shoes stay on. David wraps Amy's hair around his hand, pulls her head back gently. Amy turns to look at him, he pushes her face away)

DAVID: Don't look at me.

(Amy looks at David again. More violently this time--)

DAVID: I SAID don't look at me.

(David pulls a black satin rope from his pocket. He crosses Amy's hands in front of her and binds them with the rope.)

DAVID: Does this hurt? Shake your head yes or no.

(Amy shakes her head. No. David pulls them tighter. Amy winces)

DAVID: This?

(Amy nods her head. Yes.)

DAVID: Let's review the rules before we begin. Your safe word is "birdie". If it gets too much for you, at any time, you yell out "birdie" and I promise you that I'll stop no matter where we are. However, other than that word, you are not to speak. You are not to cry out unless you absolutely have to, in which case you should fully expect to be punished for your disobedience. If you speak or cry out frequently enough to give me cause to believe that you're doing it to deliberately irritate me, I will tie you to the bed and leave you there until you can learn to be an obedient slave. Understand?

(Amy nods again. Yes.)

(David sits on the bed, snaps his fingers, and motions for Amy to bend over his lap. She does so. He spanks her once, hard. She doesn't cry out. He spanks her again, hard. She doesn't cry out. He spanks her one more time, she almost cries out but manages to suppress it.)

DAVID: Good girl.

(David begins to caress Amy more lovingly now, almost as if to soothe the pain he has just inflicted. David walks Amy over to the bed. David kisses her passionately, but gently, and then ties her wrists to the bedframe above her head. He kisses her again. As he takes his clothes off and gets into bed. Lights up on Mona's room. Mona speaks.)

MONA: There are mornings I still reach for you
I turn over and sling my arm over what my heart remembers as your sleeping body
And it falls with a thud on the mattress.

Five minutes.
I'd give it all to have five minutes with you
Five minutes to kiss you before illness took the light
from your face.
To see myself through your eyes, to look at you and
know I was loved.
You don't think of these things when you think of being alone
How suddenly you are meaningless.
How suddenly you have stopped existing.

Five minutes for...oh who am I kidding?
Five minutes for you to tear my clothes off, put yourself safely inside me, away from strangers, away from
the world, away, away, away...
Love, I fear I am lost and am never returning.

*(Lights come back up to half on Amy in bed with David,
still in black bra and panties. David is sound asleep.
Amy gets her things, slips her dress back on. She checks
to see that David is asleep. When she's sure that he is,
she opens up a drawer in his bedside table, rummages
around for a moment. David stirs, Amy stays statue still.
When he is quiet again, Amy resumes her search and
finds a photograph. She looks at it, ashen and bewildered. Amy slips the photograph in her purse and exits.)*

Scene 3

(Julie is sitting with Maddie at a café, holding two large iced coffees. She hands one to Maddie)

MADDIE: Thanks.

JULIE: So, I wanted to talk to you outside of like…my bedroom for once.

MADDIE: Why? Because you just can't stop thinking about me?

JULIE: Be serious, Madison.

MADDIE: Awww. Look at you and your cute serious voice!

JULIE: Look. —This has been great.

MADDIE: But..?

JULIE: I think it's best that we leave it there.

MADDIE: Why?

JULIE: First of all, I'm much too old for you.

MADDIE: Okay, how old ARE you, anyway?

JULIE: Thirty four.

MADDIE: Is that all? The way you talk, it seems like you're the crypt keeper or something.

JULIE: I'm old enough to think about what's best for you.

MADDIE: Well, what about what's best for you?

JULIE: I've never been good at knowing what's best for me. That's part of the problem.

MADDIE: Does it help if I tell you that I really, really, really like you?

JULIE: I sort of figured that out.

MADDIE: What's the worst thing that can happen here? Seriously. We date for a while and then break up? That doesn't seem so bad.

JULIE: That's a very young thing to say.
Maddie, are you out?
(Maddie doesn't respond)
I thought not.
(Maddie stays quiet)
That's kind of a dealbreaker for me, to be honest.

MADDIE: I'm not like, hiding it, or anything. I just haven't been super explicit.

JULIE: But your family doesn't know.

MADDIE: Shit, I don't know. Maybe. My mom might know. It's just that we've been going through some stuff--

JULIE: What about your father? Does he know?

MADDIE: My father's dead. Hence the stuff.

JULIE: Oh.

MADDIE: Yeah. Two years ago.

JULIE: I'm sorry.

MADDIE: It's okay. I mean, well, it's not okay. It sucked.

JULIE: My dad died too. A long time ago...but still. I know what you're going through. My mom was a disaster afterwards, for years.

MADDIE: Listen, I'll tell her eventually. Unless, of course, there's someone really, really special in my life and I just HAVE to tell her.

JULIE: There's nothing I can say that will convince you, is there?

MADDIE: Not likely.

(They kiss)

MADDIE: So can we see each other again then, right? Like maybe an actual date?

(Amy enters, harried. She walks over to Julie's table. She sees Julie and Maddie being close. Julie notices Amy and backs away from Maddie)

JULIE: Amy! Hi!

AMY: Hi.

JULIE: Amy, you remember Mad—

AMY: Maddie. Of course. Nice to see you.

MADDIE: You too.

AMY: Glad you finally let her out of the house long enough to hang out.

JULIE: Amy.

AMY: I thought someone had kidnapped her or something.

MADDIE: Lord knows I tried!

(Amy sits next to Julie and takes a sip of Julie's coffee. She looks at Maddie)

AMY: Listen sweetie, I don't want to be rude or whatever, but I kind of need to talk to Julie alone.

MADDIE: Oh.

AMY: Yeah. It's a grown up thing. Nothing that would interest you.

JULIE: Ignore her. She's being a bitch. She does it very well.

MADDIE: It's okay. I should probably be getting home anyway.

JULIE: I'll call you later.

MADDIE: Not good enough. I want to see you. When can I see you?

JULIE: Tonight? I'm not doing anything.

MADDIE: Dinner?

JULIE: Sounds good. I'll pick you up at 7, okay?

MADDIE: Okay.

(*Maddie pulls Julie in for a lingering kiss, until Amy is visibly uncomfortable. Maddie looks at Amy and smiles*)

MADDIE: She's all yours.

(*Maddie exits.*)

JULIE: Was that necessary?

AMY: What?

JULIE: "Grown up thing"? Really?

AMY: It was a joke!

JULIE: It's not funny. I like her, okay?

AMY: All right, all right! Jeez. Sorry.

JULIE: So? What's up?

AMY: Um…well…

JULIE: Let me take a wild guess – this is about the guy you're seeing, right?

AMY: Kind of. Well, we're not like, dating or whatever.

JULIE: It's just some weird sex thing, right?

AMY: Why the judgment?

JULIE: Sorry.
(Beat)
    I'm listening.

AMY: It was crazy. I've never been with a guy who...I don't know. Who did to me what he did. Shook me up.

JULIE: So you like him?

AMY: He's nice. Whatever. It's just--
(Beat)
    When he was sleeping the other night, I went through his stuff.

JULIE: What?

AMY: I know. Not my proudest moment, not by a long shot...

JULIE: And?

AMY: I found something...

JULIE: What?

AMY: I think there might be another woman. Or was one...

JULIE: Divorced, maybe?

AMY: No...I don't think so. Gone, though. Dead, maybe...

JULIE: Oh come on. Why on earth would you think that...

(Amy takes the photo from her purse and shows it to Julie. Julie is stunned, recoils.)

JULIE: Oh. Oh my god.

AMY: See?

(Julie puts the photo back on the table)

JULIE: Ugh. That gives me the shivers.

AMY: He wasn't fucking me…he was…..
(Beat)
   Maybe I'm reading too much into it?

JULIE: Based on that picture? No. That woman is your twin.

AMY: It was the best sex of my life, Julie. I'm not kidding.

JULIE: Thanks a lot!

AMY: Sorry. It was though. I'm just being honest.

JULIE: Let's say you're right. Let's say that girl in the photo who happens to look exactly fucking like you is actually dead or missing and he's sleeping with you to…I don't know…fill a void. That's not healthy. In any way. That's just--

AMY: I think I want to see him again.

JULIE: I don't like this one bit.

AMY: Forget it. I shouldn't have told you.

JULIE: You wouldn't have told me if you didn't have a bad feeling about it. And you should. Because, TO REVIEW, you look exactly like some dead chick and that's fucking creepy.

AMY: Fine, okay. I won't call him. You're totally right. It was just...exciting.

JULIE: Dangerous things are always exciting. Do not call him. Ever.

(Amy and Julie get up to exit. They begin walking out as Mona and David enter. Amy sees David and freezes in place. David sees Amy. Julie exits. Mona walks in and claims a table. David and Amy lock eyes but say nothing even though Amy smiles slightly. David walks past her and goes to Mona's table. Amy exits, bewildered.)

DAVID: I'm gonna go order us coffees.
(Mona goes into her purse for money)
No, no, my treat.

MONA: Oh, thank you. I'll have a skim iced mocha. No whipped cream. Thank you!

(David exits. Mona takes out her phone and dials.)

MONA: *(on the phone)* Hey Maddie...it's Mama...I suppose I should have texted you rather than calling, but...anyway...I wanted to tell you I'm out having a coffee with someone from group. I thought you'd be proud of me for getting out of the house.... anyway, this friend is sort of...like me in a lot of ways. It's a friend, anyway...which is good. I haven't made new friends since...
(Beat. A moment.)

Okay, my darling. I'm sorry to ramble. Please text me later and let me know you're okay. I love you. Be safe…whatever you're doing.

(Mona flips the phone shut. After a moment, David returns with two enormous iced coffees.)

MONA: That looks so good. Thanks.

DAVID: Sometimes I think I might as well have a milk-shake.

MONA: You okay? That was intense today.

DAVID: Ugh. I'm sorry about that. I kind of lost my shit.

MONA: Don't be. It was honest.

DAVID: Everyone says this is supposed to get easier with time. In some ways, I feel like it's gotten harder.

MONA: It only gets easier when you start to forget things. That's the only way we mortals survive, right? Forgetting.
(Checks her phone)
I have no idea where my daughter is.

DAVID: How old is she again?

MONA: Nineteen.

DAVID: You don't look old enough to have a nineteen year old.

MONA: Thank you. Some days I feel absolutely fucking ancient.

DAVID: Me too. It scares me sometimes, you know? I'm thirty five and alone.

MONA: Try being forty two. And a woman, no less.

DAVID: You don't look a day over thirty. Seriously.

MONA: Well, thank you. I certainly work very hard at it.

DAVID: Most women wouldn't admit that.

MONA: I've resigned myself to a life of skim milk and injectables.

DAVID: Botox?

MONA: Can you tell?

DAVID: No!

MONA: When Maddie turned thirteen. I had a meltdown of epic proportions. I felt old and unattractive, and Richard, ever the pragmatist, said that if it would really make me feel better, he'd support it.

DAVID: Did it make you feel better?

MONA: Not really. But it got the crow's feet and wrinkles to slow down a tick. That's all I wanted, really. It's like a bag of chips, though. Once you get one thing done, well, you gotta eat the rest of the bag...or something.
(Beat)
I'm embarrassed now.

DAVID: Don't be. I like listening to you. It makes me feel less...well, less alone. I often feel like I'm from a different planet than everyone else.

MONA: I do too. I can't even hang out with my friends anymore. They're all married, and they keep telling me "It's been two years, you need to date, move on". And I'm always so confused by that. I mean, if they lost each other...would the first thing on their agenda be to date someone else?

(David doesn't reply)

MONA: Oh, are you dating? That was probably offensive if you are, I'm sorry.

DAVID: No. Well. No. Not exactly.

MONA: No?

DAVID: It's just--

MONA: Sex?

DAVID: Right.

MONA: How's that working out for you?

DAVID: It's uh...well, it's...this girl I'm currently uh, seeing is...well, she's--
(Beat)
All I can see is Ashley.

MONA: That's why I've just avoided it outright.

DAVID: There's been no one? Since Richard?
(Mona shakes her head)
Wow. That's—

MONA: Pathetic.

DAVID: No. It's kind of romantic, actually.

MONA: I just can't. I tried, once, with this friend of
mine, and…I saw Richard's face. It felt like lying.

DAVID: I guess that's my problem. I just let myself lie.

MONA: I guess it's that I just feel so separate from my
own body now -- like someone has torn me into
pieces and tossed my limbs in the air. I'm just shim-
mying around with no arms or legs trying to find
them, but I don't have any hands, and I can't pick
them up.

DAVID: Humpty Dumpty, off the wall.

MONA: Exactly.

(David raises his cup to Mona)

DAVID: Well, here's to all the king's horses and all the
king's men. For at least trying.
(They clink cups)
Cheers.

DAVID: Thanks for inviting me out. I'm actually having a good time.

MONA: Well, then we should make this a tradition. If
we're going to suffer through group, there might as
well be mochas involved.

DAVID: You think I can go back in there after all that?

MONA: Of course. You're *grieving*, poor dear. You know not what you do.

DAVID: Get Out of Jail Free.

MONA: Exactly.

DAVID: It's a deal.

(LIGHTS OUT)

Scene 4

(David is sitting on his bed. There is a knock on David's door. He answers. It's Amy, in the same black dress. She smiles.)

AMY: Hi, David.

(David puts a finger to her lips to hush her. Obediently, Amy wordlessly undresses and crosses her arms in front of her to be tied. David takes great sensual pleasure in tying her wrists together. He puts her into position on the bed and reveals a long, thin riding crop. Amy can barely conceal her fear and desire. He smacks her once, and then twice, and the lights go down on them for the third audible smack. Lights come up on Julie's bedroom, where Julie and Maddie are cuddling, half-dressed)

MADDIE: Jules?

JULIE: Hmmm?

MADDIE: Why don't you sculpt anymore?

JULIE: I dunno. What's it to ya?

MADDIE: I keep thinking about that piece you made that you showed me. It's so beautiful.

JULIE: You know what else is beautiful? Sleeping.

MADDIE: I could never make anything like that.

JULIE: Sure you could.

MADDIE: No. That requires talent. I'm not talented at anything.

JULIE: Everyone is talented at something.

MADDIE: Why did you quit?

JULIE: I realized there were about a million people who were younger and better than I was. Not saying I was totally unsuccessful, or anything. I had some shows. I sold some pieces. But I was a salmon swimming upstream, for years, and one day I just stopped swimming. Simple as that.

MADDIE: But you were good.

JULIE: Good has less to do with it than you think.

MADDIE: I can't even draw a stick figure.

JULIE: Come on. 'Fess up. What are you good at?

MADDIE: I dunno…

JULIE: There has to be something.

MADDIE: Math.

JULIE: See! That's something. Not everyone is good at math. I suck at math.

MADDIE: Math is boring though. I feel like a dork even telling you.

JULIE: Math is not boring. Math gives an answer to nearly every question it asks. Art is nothing but asking questions and there's never an answer.

MADDIE: Math can't answer why I'm gay.

JULIE: Do you wish you weren't?

MADDIE: Maybe?

JULIE: Really?

MADDIE: I dunno. Sometimes? It just makes everything really complicated.

JULIE: Everything is complicated.

MADDIE: I guess. But straight people come with instructions. Slot A fits into Slot B. Marry, procreate…

JULIE: Hang on there, missy. We can do both those things. Well…in a few states anyway. But babies? Babies we can do.

MADDIE: Yeah but…if you have your own, it's not both of yours, you know? And if you adopt, it doesn't belong to either of you.

JULIE: I cannot believe you think that matters.

MADDIE: I just…I guess I've never understood how you can look at a child and call it yours when you didn't create it, is all. Of course you can love it, and raise it, but you always know that it's not your flesh and blood.

JULIE: If you found out tomorrow that your dad wasn't your biological father, would he be any less your dad?

MADDIE: To tell me that wasn't true would be like telling me I don't exist. I'm not as sure of anything as I am sure that I'm my father's child.

JULIE: But he wouldn't be any less your father. He'd still be the man who held your hand crossing the street or gushing over some scribbly picture you drew him when you were little.

MADDIE: What if you found out your dad wasn't really your dad?

JULIE: I'd buy everyone a beer.

MADDIE: What do you mean?

(Julie shows Maddie a spot on her temple)

JULIE: See this scar? White, sort of moon shaped…
(Maddie nods)
Not everyone had what you had.

MADDIE: I'm sorry.

JULIE: Don't be. Ancient history.

(They fall silent)

MADDIE: I would never lay a hand on you, you know.

JULIE: Stay there.

MADDIE: For what?

(Julie takes out a pencil and notebook)

JULIE: I'm going to sketch you.

MADDIE: Like Jack and Rose in *Titanic*?

(Maddie lays on the bed like Kate Winslet in Titanic, arm over her head. She poses dramatically.)

JULIE: I hate that movie.

MADDIE: How can you hate that movie?

JULIE: Stay still.

MADDIE: I thought you were just a paralegal.

JULIE: I still draw sometimes. Only when I'm inspired.

MADDIE: I inspire you?

JULIE: Maybe a little.

MADDIE: "Draw me like one of your French girls, Jack…"

JULIE: Hush.

(Julie sketches. A moment of quiet)

MADDIE: What's your favorite color?

JULIE: Why do you ask so many questions?
(Maddie pouts)
  Blue.

MADDIE: Blue like the sky or blue like the ocean?

JULIE: The ocean – but not like the Caribbean, or the Pacific. Like the Atlantic…the Northeast…opaque and deep and mysterious. Almost grey, wild and endless.

(Julie puts the sketchbook down)

MADDIE: Can I see it?

JULIE: It's not done!

MADDIE: I want to see.

JULIE: You need to learn to be more patient.

(Julie puts the sketchbook away, distracts Maddie by touching her)

JULIE: Maybe one day I'll make a sculpture again. Maybe it will be you.

MADDIE: A nude?

(Julie kisses Maddie, runs her hands over her body)

JULIE: I'm going to need to touch you some more. Easier to sculpt the curve of someone's hip when you've felt it with your bare hands.

(Maddie slides Julie's shirt off, kisses her stomach, her chest, her lips again)

MADDIE: I love how you get all red when I do that.

JULIE: I flush easily.

MADDIE: You're the most beautiful thing I've ever seen.

JULIE: And you're going to break my heart.

MADDIE: Never. Never ever.

JULIE. Never is a promise.

MADDIE: Isn't that a song?

JULIE: Yes.

MADDIE: Fiona Apple.

JULIE: Yes.

MADDIE: I love that song.

JULIE: Me too.

MADDIE: I love you.

JULIE: Don't say that.

MADDIE: I mean it.

JULIE: Sssh. Stop talking.

(Maddie begins to undress, their bed is obscured in darkness as lights come up on David's bed, where Amy is being untied from the bedposts. She is, again, only in black underwear and bra. We can tell that her legs have been whipped or spanked – angry red welts appear on them. When David has finished untying her, Amy involuntarily throws her arms around him. David holds her for a long minute, remembers, and then lets her go. The switch has flipped. David has turned himself off again).

DAVID: Are you okay? Nod yes or no.

(Amy nods)

DAVID: Are you hurt?

(Amy shakes her head "no")

DAVID: Do you need a ride home?

(Amy shakes her head "no")

DAVID: Okay. I'll let you alone so you can get dressed.
   Thanks for uh…I mean…

(Amy nods. David exits. Amy is emotional as she begins
to put her clothes on – black skirt, black top. Amy slides
the skirt over her legs, and smarts when it hits the welts.
Amy examines them. Amy gets her purse, retrieves her
cell phone. She dials. The lights come up softly on Julie
and Maddie in bed, who are sleeping. Julie answers the
phone after a few rings. Maddie sits up behind her, kissing her neck and back as she speaks)

JULIE: Amy?

AMY: Hey! Hey uh…can you meet me for a drink?

JULIE: It's late.

AMY: I need to talk to you. Now.

JULIE: I'm busy.

AMY: You with her?

MADDIE: Baby, come on…

AMY: (Mocking) "Babyyyy come on…".

JULIE: If I agree to meet you, will you shut up?

AMY: Yes.

JULIE: Fine.

AMY: 20 minutes?

JULIE: All right.

AMY: Text me when you're on your way.

(Amy hangs up. Alone, in the dark, she finishes getting dressed. Julie is getting dressed. Maddie is annoyed.)

MADDIE: You can't just do whatever she wants all the time.

JULIE: She's my best friend.

MADDIE: She's your ex girlfriend.

JULIE: Not really. We just slept together a couple of times. I was like her lesbian lab rat.

MADDIE: Do you still love her?

JULIE: I'm with you, Maddie. You're just going to have to trust that.
(Julie looks at Maddie, who is hurt.)
C'mon. You should get home anyway.

MADDIE: I don't have a fucking curfew.

(Maddie grabs her bag)

JULIE: What are you gonna do, walk?

MADDIE: I'll be fine.

JULIE: Maddie…come on.

MADDIE: Don't tell me what to do.

(Maddie exits. Lights fade on the bedrooms.)

Scene 5

(Amy is waiting for Julie at the café. Amy is still wearing a skirt, and the marks on her legs are obvious. She keeps self-consciously pulling it down. Julie enters, looking angry, but sees Amy and immediately softens, though her voice stays hard.)

JULIE: Well. I'm here.

AMY: Hi.

JULIE: What's going on?
(Amy doesn't say anything)
    Might I remind you that you dragged me away from a truly excellent evening to come all the way here?

AMY: I know.

JULIE: I know you don't like, CARE or anything, but I was having a really good time and she's off somewhere in a huff walking home by herself and I just--

(Amy shows the welts to Julie.)

JULIE What the hell is that?

(Amy doesn't answer)

JULIE: He did this to you?

(Amy nods)

JULIE: I thought you said you were going to stop seeing him!

AMY: I thought I could.

JULIE: This stuff is dangerous! Even with someone you know, never mind some grief stricken psychopath you met on the fucking internet!

AMY: I don't need a lecture right now.

JULIE: Clearly you do!
(Softens)
Your legs are a mess. What did he—

AMY: Riding crop.

JULIE: Jesus.

AMY: It's not as bad as it looks.

JULIE: Then why are you so upset?

AMY: I can't talk to him.

JULIE: You can't talk to him?

AMY: He asked me not to. I mean, I CAN, right? It's not like illegal but we have rules, and anyway, talking is for logistics and planning. I would never talk to him about my feelings, or anything.
(Beat)
Jules? When you and I were…you know…why wouldn't you…even when I asked you, begged you, you simply wouldn't and I just—

JULIE: You know why.

AMY: But if it meant we could have been together—

JULIE: We couldn't have been together.

AMY: Why? Why not?

JULIE: Because you're not actually gay, Amy!

AMY: So what? Does it really matter all that much?

JULIE: Yes! It totally matters!

AMY: But maybe, maybe if you could have given me what I needed…just sometimes, it doesn't have to be all the time for me to--

JULIE: I just couldn't. I couldn't hurt you on purpose. Ever. You know that. Besides, I needed things too. Like a girlfriend who wanted to have sex with me.

AMY: I was working on it!

JULIE: You can't *work* on something like that, Ames! You either want to do it or you don't.
(Beat)
I'm not judging you. We all need things. But you can get what you need without all of this…insanity. Someone who's going to love you.

AMY: I had someone who loved me. And I threw it all away.

JULIE: Ugh. Stop it. You always do this.

AMY: Do what?

JULIE: Act like you're all torn up that we're not together. It's crap. It's like getting me to whip you without the leather.

AMY: We could have been happy.

JULIE: You dumped *me*, remember! Hello?

AMY: Maybe it was a mistake?
(Beat)
I dunno. I'm just asking you to understand.

JULIE: No. You're asking me to give you permission. And I can't. This is your choice.

AMY: Like it's your choice to date some lovesick teen-ager, right?

JULIE: Don't change the subject.

AMY: You know, maybe that's not like, the most well adjusted thing on earth either! Ever think of that?

JULIE: Yes, actually. I think of that every day. But I'm not hurting her.

AMY: I'm not getting hurt.

JULIE: Even if that were true, who's to say you're not hurting him, Amy? You might be doing more harm than good by playing along with his strange little game.

AMY: I don't want to hurt him. I just want to be that person for him, even if it's just for that short time…

JULIE: Well you're not. You don't even know what happened to her.
(Beat)
I have to go.

(Julie exits.)

(Lights out)

Scene 6

(Lights up on David. He is sitting on his bed)

DAVID: I remember the first real day without you.
The funeral was over, your folks had left.
My folks had left.
Our friends had left.
The police had left.
I woke up on our couch and I couldn't go back into our bed yet.
The sheets hadn't been changed, and I knew I'd pull back the duvet and be smacked in the face with the smell of you, and I knew that it would kill me.
For some reason, I didn't want to die.
It's funny how we survive.

I made myself a bowl of cereal, brewed a pot of coffee
I sat down at our table, in the same spot,
I swear I waited for you to walk in, muss my hair, say "silly boy", as if making breakfast could somehow bring you back, as if I could defeat death with routine.

By the time I got the courage to go back in there, it had been long months
It had been so long that our bedroom had developed cobwebs.
I tore back the duvet and was wrecked to find that your smell was gone.
I pressed my nose against the sheets, desperate for even the hint of your perfume, but you were gone, and just like that, I lost you all over again.
So I went to a bar, got incredibly drunk, and the pretty bartender took pity on me.
In her apartment, I fucked her, nearly hysterical with pleasure and grief,

52

And in her drunken haze, she asked me to spank her.
So I did.
Hard.
I looked down and saw my handprint materialize on her skin like a developing photo

And suddenly, for one moment, you were there, my love.
Tossing your hair back, red as she was, red on white, until it blurred before me
And as I left her apartment at daybreak
I felt alive, and full of possibility
There was a way to bring you back.
There was finally a way.
So, I've been chasing your ghost under the skirts of strangers.
Until there was her.

(Amy knocks, David opens the door. Amy enters)

(On one side of the stage, Amy and David are in David's bedroom. On the other, Maddie and Julie are in Maddie's house on the couch. During the course of this scene things heat up on both sides of the stage. Lights come up on Amy and David. Amy, following their established "sex rules", starts to unzip her dress. David stops her and removes it for her instead. Amy is confused by this. Lights up on Julie and Maddie. They are making-out on the sofa. Julie takes Maddie's shirt off.)

JULIE: Are you sure your mother isn't coming home? I feel weird...

MADDIE: She said she was going to my aunt's house... not coming back until tomorrow.

JULIE: Are you sure?

MADDIE: I'm positive.

(Maddie kisses Julie. They continue kissing quietly while on the other side of the stage, Amy tries to continue the sex-game. Amy puts her hands in front of her to be bound. Instead of being bound, David takes her hand and kisses it softly. Julie pulls out of her kiss with Maddie.)

JULIE: Should we go to your room?

MADDIE: I want you right now.

(Maddie kisses Julie – they continue to make out. They continue kissing quietly while...
David looks Amy in the face and kisses Amy tenderly. Amy looks stunned.
Julie stops the kiss and says...)

JULIE: Do you have any idea how sexy you are?

MADDIE: No.

JULIE: You are.

MADDIE: Show me.

(Maddie pulls Julie back into her embrace and things heat up. At the same time, on the other side of the stage, David lifts Amy up in his arms and lays her down on the bed. He does not tie her, rather lays on top her and kisses her. Amy is unsure of what to do.)

MADDIE: You feel so good...

DAVID: You feel so good...

JULIE: Kiss me.

AMY: What are you—

(Julie and Maddie are kissing and in various stages of sexual activity during the whole scene. It should be passionate and tender. This goes on for a while without anyone saying anything, until...)

DAVID: Ssssh...
So perfect
My perfect girl.

AMY: I can't feel my arm—

DAVID: Sssh. It's okay. It's okay.

AMY: Oh god—

DAVID: I love you.

AMY: This is—I'm not--

DAVID: It's okay.

(David is lost somewhere. Amy recoils, squirms in her restraints)

(Dialogue starts again)

JULIE: Did you hear something?

MADDIE: No.

JULIE: I heard something.

AMY: Okay...stop.

55

MADDIE: Come on, don't stop--

DAVID: Sssh...stop talking...

JULIE: Sorry.

AMY: I'm scared.

MADDIE: I'm so close.

DAVID: It's okay...

JULIE: Okay. Okay sorry—

AMY: Don't!

DAVID: Please.

(They start again, Maddie cries out.)

MADDIE: Yes!

AMY: I WANT YOU TO STOP.

DAVID: What?

AMY: I'M HERE AND I AM SCARED JUST STOP! FUCKING STOP IT!!

DAVID: I—

(There is the noise of car keys, a door handle)

JULIE: Shit. Someone's trying to open the door!

AMY: YOU ARE HURTING ME. PLEASE STOP NOW! DAVID STOP IT, PLEASE!

(Mona enters. The two women frantically try to cover themselves. Mona flips on the light.)

(David stops, stunned. Amy is halfway between crying and hyperventilating.)

(Mona is standing in the doorway with a large paper bag with handles. Maddie and Julie are deer caught in the headlights)

MONA: Maddie?

MADDIE: Mama!

JULIE: Oh my god.

MONA: Hi. I got Chinese.

(Mona lifts the bag. Lights down.)

ACT TWO

Scene 1

(Maddie and Julie are now fully dressed and sitting as far apart from one another as humanly possible. Julie is sheepish, humiliated. Maddie has the scowl of a grounded thirteen year old. Mona, despite her internal struggle, is obstinately chipper.)

MONA: Well, aren't you going to stay for dinner?

JULIE: Am I?

MONA: I feel like we should get to know each other a bit more...formally, don't you?

MADDIE: Mother!

MONA: You do not get to "mother" me right now. Not even a little.

JULIE: I'm sorry about this, Mrs. Archer. Really. I am.

MONA: You know, normally I'd ask you to call me Mona, but it's been a long time since anyone called me Mrs. Archer. I'm keeping it.
(Begins unpacking the Chinese food from the bag)
You like Kung Pao Chicken? Butterfly shrimp?

MADDIE: Julie's a vegetarian.

MONA: Well, of course she is. I got veggie lo mein--

JULIE: I don't think I should--

MONA: Oh, don't be silly! Keeping up with my daughter must have you positively famished.
(Holds up a bag)
Crispy noodles? Duck sauce?

MADDIE: Why are you being rude?

MONA: Rude? Oh, by rude you must mean having sex on my couch with someone I've never even heard of!

JULIE: Maddie said you were out for the night, and—

MONA: Did she?

JULIE: That doesn't make it right. It's not her house—

MADDIE: It's not?

JULIE: I'm so sorry.

MONA: It's not your fault.
(Pause)
Of all the things not to know about your own kid…

MADDIE: I wanted to tell you. I was going to.

MONA: When?

MADDIE: When I was sure…when I was sure that I was—

(Mona digs into her food)

MONA: Ooh. Spicy.
(Puts the container down, gets up)
You know what? I could use a big glass of wine. Anyone else? I'd hate to drink alone…I'll go grab it.

(Mona exits. Julie is incensed)

JULIE: This is...this is just

MADDIE: She was supposed to be out!

JULIE: How awful for her to find out like this--

MADDIE: She's being such a drama queen.

JULIE: Do you have any conception of what she must be feeling right now? At all?

MADDIE: It's always about what she's feeling.

JULIE: Well, it's been fun, but I think I've been sufficiently humiliated for one evening.

(Julie stands to leave, grabs her purse. Maddie follows as Julie heads for the door)

MADDIE: You're leaving?

JULIE: No offense, but it would be a little bit weird to eat Chinese food with the woman who just caught me fucking her teenage daughter on the couch.

MADDIE: So that's what you think of me then? Just some teenager you're fucking?
(Julie doesn't answer)
I love you. Does that matter to you? At all?

JULIE: I have to go.

MADDIE: No you don't.

JULIE: Oh, yes I do. What *planet* do you live on, Maddie? What made you think this was okay?

(Julie exits.)

MONA: *(Still offstage)*
I hope you like Riesling…it's all we have…
(Mona re-enters, holding an open bottle of white and three glasses)
…goes well with Asian.
(Pause)
Where'd she go?

MADDIE: She left.

MONA: Oh.
(Sees Maddie's anger)
Are you drinking, or what?
(Mona splits the entire bottle of wine into two glasses)
Well, here it is if you want it.
(Mona takes a large sip)
Are you going to speak, or do I have to do all the talking here?

MADDIE: What do you want me to say?

MONA: I don't know.
(Maddie picks up the glass and drinks)
How long have you…I mean…are you sure that—

MADDIE: A long time.

MONA: Did your father know?
(Maddie doesn't answer)
He did.
(Maddie drinks)
He never said anything to me.

MADDIE: I made him promise.

MONA: He never kept anything from me.

MADDIE: You weren't the only one he had allegiances to, you know.

MONA: Oh, Maddie, of course not. He loved you terribly.
(Beat)
I'm sorry if I embarrassed you. I didn't know how to…
(Beat)
…how OLD is she, anyway?

MADDIE: Okay, I'm done talking about this if you're going to judge me.

MONA: I'm not judging you!

MADDIE: You judge everyone! All the time! Why do you think I didn't want to tell you?

MONA: I don't care that you're a lesbian, Maddie! I care that you didn't trust me enough to tell me something so important!

MADDIE: You honestly didn't suspect?

MONA: I guess I wasn't paying that close of attention.

MADDIE: Obviously.

MONA: So this is all my fault, then? I'm a terrible mother, so you're running around sleeping with god knows who and doing god knows what? Fine. But you

don't talk to me anymore, Maddie. How am I supposed to know anything about anything when you
don't talk to me?

MADDIE: I try to talk to you! But all you do is sit in
that stupid room and drink wine and fold your stupid
birds.
(Beat)
Fuck it. This is pointless.

(Maddie grabs her stuff and exits)

MONA: It's too late for you to be going out! Maddie—

*(Maddie doesn't come back. Mona takes her wine into
her office, the room with all the birds. Mona takes out a
piece of origami paper and begins folding a crane.)*

MONA: Each fold is precise, calculated
    A quarter of a centimeter off and it's over
    If you fold an origami crane wrong, it looks stupid
    Misshapen, alien.
    So beautiful, yet rigid
    Unmoveable, slim margins of error
    If you fail, it is because of your folly
    Your humanity.
    It's not like other art – ethereal, subjective, fluid.
    This is the way it is done
    The way it has always been done
    The way it will always be done.
    And any deviation is a reflection on you.

    It's the creasing that really matters.
    Making each fold count.
    Folding forward and back and forward and back
    And back…and forward…

(Beat)

...how could you keep something like that from me?

The one thing I've ever really created, and I don't recognize her.

What we made together, what can't be undone, is my undoing?

Where did I go wrong that you both kept me in the dark?

What step did I skip?

What crease wasn't creased?

Help me.

God, someone, anyone.

Help me.

Scene 2

(Amy and David are still in his bedroom. Amy's hair is a mess. Neither are looking at one another. Amy is half dressed. David looks terrified, but stays silent. He is sitting on the edge of the bed, staring into space.)

AMY: Am I allowed to speak now?
(David doesn't respond)
   I guess so since I kind of, uh, ended the scene.
(Pause)
   I forgot the safe word. I'm sorry about that. I panicked. It happens. No biggie, right?
(David doesn't respond)
   Mind if I smoke?
(David makes a face but doesn't say anything.)
   There's the benefit of you being the strong silent type. I'll ash in this glass. I promise I'll clean it before I leave.

(Amy gets out of bed, finds a shirt, throws it on. She sits in the chair, lights her cigarette that she retrieves from her purse. She inhales thoughtfully, exhales loudly. She starts talking way too fast.)

AMY: I don't normally smoke. I keep a pack in my purse. I find that I go to them when I'm feeling socially awkward. You know, in a bar or whatever. I hate being in a room full of people. I dunno…I'm really a social person but I find it hard to make the first move. You know, initiate conversation. I always find that the friends I make are with the people I meet outside smoking at bars. They're usually, I dunno, like…immediately interesting. Like, maybe they're not really but maybe I'm just attracted to people who do something, like, blatantly unhealthy. Like, you've gotta be kind of fucked in the head to enjoy lighting some dead nasty leaves on fire and inhaling them and not even getting high or anything. You know? So I keep them with me to make friends. Wow. I make friends giving myself lung cancer! That just makes me a big hot mess, doesn't it? At least I don't smoke Newports...now those are disgusting, a friend of mine smokes them and the stench is positively vile...

DAVID: *(Suddenly, forcefully)* I mind.

AMY: What?

(David yanks the lit cigarette from her hand, extinguishes it)

DAVID: I mind. I mind you smoking. I don't smoke.

AMY: I ASKED you, you know. You could have... you could have SAID, you know, like....talking....where you open your mouth and words come out--

DAVID: Oh and you know ALL about that, don't you? You never seem to stop doing that even though it's the one fucking thing I asked you not to do!

AMY: Oh, excuse me! I'm sorry!
(Begins gathering her things, getting dressed. By the end of the scene she's fully dressed and ready to go.)
I didn't know these stupid rules applied outside of the scene, you know. I mean, I get that this is like, you know, an agreement. I need something, you need something, all good. But Jesus...I do whatever you want. Whatever you say. And you don't give a shit. You won't even talk to me.

DAVID: I just can't be...available. To you. To anyone.

AMY: I'm not asking for a relationship. Hell, that's the last thing I want. I'm just saying, would a few seconds of small talk really break the illusion that much?

DAVID: Illusion?

AMY: The resemblance *is* uncanny, I've got to give you that. I mean, I saw that picture and was like…wow, hey sister, stop swimming in my gene pool--

DAVID: How did you—

AMY: I knew something weird was going on, so I looked around and found her picture.

DAVID: How long? How long have you--

AMY: Since the beginning.

DAVID: What was I saying, before? What scared you?

AMY: You said "I love you".

(David's reaction resembles the crumpling of a piece of paper)

AMY: I believed you. In that moment. And I felt it and it scared the shit out of me.

DAVID: I feel like I should be apologizing and that doesn't seem quite…enough, I guess.

AMY: Look. It's okay. All out in the open, right? Whew! Everyone can relax and it's not so weird and…we can just get on with it!

DAVID: Get on with it?

(There is a long silence. Finally--)
   I think you should probably go.

AMY: Yeah. It's getting pretty late.

DAVID: I think we should stop seeing each other.

AMY: What? Why?

DAVID: I think that's fairly obvious.

AMY: Oh. Okay. So you get to make all the decisions here, is that it?

DAVID: No. It's just…this isn't--

AMY: If I never said anything?

(Beat)

DAVID: Do you need cab fare?

AMY: Um, I do, like, own a car. I'm not some dead-beat…

DAVID: I never said you—

AMY: I have a job, okay? I'm a certified public accountant, for your information! And I have a condo. A nice condo. By the waterfront! That I own!

DAVID: I just wanted to make sure that you—

AMY: That what? I didn't need a ride because I wasn't some vagabond or drug addict or something because

GOD FORBID a woman seek out kinky sex without being a complete mental case, right?

DAVID: I never thought—

AMY: I'd rather walk than take your money!

DAVID: I'm just trying to make this better.

AMY: Please. Like you give a shit. If you had, then none of this would ever—
(Beat. It's over, and she knows it)
Never mind. I'm leaving.

(Amy, now fully dressed, gets her purse, and exits without saying anything else.

Lights out)

Scene 3

(Time has passed. Mona has fallen asleep on her desk, empty glass of wine beside her. It is late. The sound of rain and distant thunder fill the space. Suddenly, the doorbell rings. Mona does not awaken. The doorbell rings again. Mona wakes up as if electrocuted.)

MONA: Maddie.

(Mona rushes to the front door and opens it. It is David, who is soaking wet.)

MONA: David!

DAVID: Hi. Can I come in?

MONA: Of course, of course.

(David enters. Mona closes the door. Mona sees that David is shaking.)

MONA: You're drenched.

DAVID: I tried to call—

MONA: Oh shit.
(Mona looks at her phone, which is on the table)
   I fell asleep.

DAVID: I woke you. I'm so sorry.

MONA: David. Are you all right?

DAVID: Not really.

MONA: This won't do. You'll freeze in those wet clothes.

(Beat)

Listen. Upstairs, in my bedroom…first door on the left…there are some men's clothes. Bottom drawer of the big chest in there. Can't miss it.

DAVID: Mona, I couldn't—

MONA: Don't be silly. Old T-shirts and pants.

DAVID: Thanks.

MONA: Don't forget to leave your wet clothes in the bathroom so I can toss them in the dryer.

(David exits. Mona retreats to the study. She opens the drawer and selects a piece of origami paper, begins to fold)

MONA: Step one.
Take a square piece of origami paper, fold it in half lengthwise.
Step two.
Unfold the paper.
Step three.
Turn the paper, fold in half again on the opposite side.
Step four.
Unfold the paper.
Step five…
What am I…
What is he…

(Mona continues folding. David approaches the door in clothing that doesn't fit him well. Mona keeps folding.)

DAVID: Mo?

MONA: In here.

(David enters the crane room. It is the first time he has seen it.)

DAVID: Wow. You make all these?

MONA: With my two little hands.

(Beat. Mona looks at David, who is wearing her late husband's clothing. A moment.)

MONA: So, what drove you here, of all places, in the pouring rain?

DAVID: I called it off with that girl I've been seeing. Sleeping with…whatever you want to call it.

MONA: I'm sorry.

DAVID: Yeah.

MONA: But it was just sex, right? I mean, that's what you told me, anyway.

DAVID: It was a little more complicated.

(David takes out his cellphone, presses some buttons, shows the phone to Mona)

DAVID: This was Ashley. The one who—

MONA: I know who Ashley is.
(Beat)
  She was so beautiful, David. Truly.

(David finds another photo)

DAVID: This is the photo that Amy sent me before we met. Amy is the girl I've been seeing.

(David shows Mona, who takes the phone)

MONA: Oh my god.
(Mona looks again)
Oh, David…

DAVID: So you see my dilemma…

MONA: How is that even possible? I mean, almost EX-ACTLY…

(David is beside himself. Mona is at an uncharacteristic loss for words)

MONA: You know what? Let's have a drink.

(David and Mona go back out into the livingroom)

MONA: I've been drinking this terrible Riesling all by myself…

DAVID: You don't have anything a little stronger, do you?

MONA: I think I have an old bottle of vodka some-where--

DAVID: Now you're talking.

(Mona goes into a cabinet and finds a bottle of vodka.)

MONA: How do you want it?

DAVID: In a glass.

(Mona pours a generous amount of vodka into the glass and hands it to a grateful David. Mona pours the rest of the bottle of wine into her glass.)

DAVID: Thank you.

MONA: So what happened?

DAVID: Amy found a photo of Ashley. I guess she's known for a while and didn't say anything about it, which made me realize that what I was doing was just... is there a stronger word than "reprehensible"?

MONA: But why'd she go along with it?
(David doesn't answer)
    David...does this woman know what happened to Ashley?

DAVID: I didn't elaborate.

MONA: Maybe she'd understand?

DAVID: I don't want her to understand. I'm completely wrong here. I like...infected her with my brokenness. I had no right.

MONA: Everyone's always infecting someone with something.

DAVID: I could infect you too, you know.

MONA: I don't know if you've noticed...but I've turned into a crazy woman who folds birds all alone in a room and drinks bottles of wine by herself.

74

DAVID: I'm sorry I barged in on you.

MONA: You can barge in on me whenever you want.

(David surveys the empty wine bottles, Chinese food containers)

DAVID: You know, I thought I was having a bad night, but you don't seem to be doing so hot, yourself.

MONA: Everything's a disaster actually. A wreck.
(Beat)
My daughter is a lesbian, as it turns out. A lesbian who hates me.

DAVID: Does it bother you that she's a lesbian?

MONA: Maybe a little? I know it shouldn't. I guess it bothers me most that I didn't know.

DAVID: Should you have?

MONA: I don't know…I guess it was just easier for me not to worry about it. Not think.

DAVID: Coming out must be really difficult. I'm sure whatever you said can be---

MONA: Oh, she didn't really come out. She BURST out, guns blazing. My daughter does nothing halfway.

(David sees a photo on the coffee table, picks it up)

DAVID: Is this her?

MONA: Yes. And Richard.

DAVID: How old was she?

MONA: About twelve.

DAVID: She really does look like him.

MONA: She talks like him too. Moves like him. Makes the same jokes. It's like I wasn't even involved in her conception. Except I was. I remember it pretty well, actually.

(David puts his arm around her. Mona rests her head on his shoulder)

DAVID: I hate that we're both here right now. But I'd rather be here than anywhere else.

(Mona looks up at David and smiles. Suddenly, impulsively, David kisses Mona. They kiss tenderly and for a long moment before it stops.)

MONA: Oh.

DAVID: I'm sorry. That was--

MONA: Inappropriately timed, maybe?

DAVID: I know! What made me—

MONA: Honestly? It felt really good.

DAVID: It did?

MONA: Fucking GREAT.

DAVID: Great?

MONA: Yes. Absolutely.

DAVID: Me too. So we're good then?

MONA: Yes.

DAVID: Can I have more vodka?

MONA: You can have the whole bottle if you want.

(Mona gets up and starts to walk away)

DAVID: Where are you going?

MONA: I'm calling it a night. We're in emotionally dangerous territory here, don't you agree?

DAVID: Are we?

MONA: Everyone in group would be VERY against this kind of behavior.

DAVID: Acting out?

MONA: Yes.

DAVID: Grieving in unhealthy ways.

MONA: Exacerbating denial.

DAVID: Not dealing with the real issues.

MONA: There are bedclothes and pillows in the linen closet next to the bathroom. You can sleep in the spare bedroom too, if you want. Up the stairs, last door on your right.

DAVID: Are you sure you don't want to stay up and drink with me?

MONA: We'll get breakfast tomorrow morning. Something brutally unhealthy. Something with hollandaise sauce.

DAVID: And mochas?

MONA: Always mochas. Good night, David.

(Mona exits. Lights fade.)

Scene 4

(Julie and Amy are at the bar again. They are both drinking some concoction in a martini glass and also have shots of something-or-other that doesn't resemble anything someone in their thirties should consider drinking. They are both reasonably drunk.)

JULIE: ...so then her MOTHER walks in...

AMY: Oh no.

JULIE: Oh yes.

AMY: What the FUCK?

JULIE: That's what I said!

AMY: What did her mom say? Did she go nuts on you?

JULIE: I felt so bad for her. She was trying so hard to be nice. She offered me wine and Chinese food. I was just so mad...

AMY: So you left.

JULIE: And now I'm here.

AMY: I'm glad. It's been a terrible fucking day.
(Amy raises her martini glass. Julie follows suit)
   To terrible fucking days!

JULIE: To being complete morons who never do ANYTHING right!
(They laugh and clink glasses)
   Are you really done with this guy though?

AMY: Yes.

JULIE: I'll believe it when I see it.

AMY: I still don't know what happened. To the girl. My twin.

JULIE: Didn't you google him?
(Amy shakes her head "no")
DUDE. Google is your friend!

AMY: I kind of don't want to know. I've made up my own little stories about her. Like…she offed herself in a bathtub of champagne by taking a bottle of Xanax. Or she simply left one day, only leaving behind some damp pantyhose and a vague note.

JULIE: You are seriously deranged.

AMY: I have an active imagination.

JULIE: Whatever. I can't talk. I was dating a teenage closet case with daddy issues.

AMY: So you finally admit you're just as fucked up as I am?

JULIE: Not a chance!

AMY: Stubborn bitch.

JULIE: I'm just so stupid. I have all these silly romantic obsessions and they always turn out to be complete failures.

AMY: Myself included?

JULIE: Especially you!

(Amy pouts)

And look at me now. I'm a hot mess.

AMY: Julie. I'm sorry I'm not gay. I really, really wanted to be.

JULIE: I know. I know you did. And you gave it your best shot.

AMY: Did I?

JULIE: You did. You tried really hard and I appreciate it.

(Julie kisses Amy on the head. Suddenly, Maddie enters, breathless. Amy sees her.)

AMY: Oh dear.

MADDIE: I thought I might find you here. And look with who…surprise, surprise.

AMY: We were just—

MADDIE: You're always JUST.

JULIE: I thought I said I'd call you tomorrow.

MADDIE: No. You didn't.

JULIE: Yes, I did. I think I answered one of your eight million texts before I turned my phone off.

MADDIE: I needed to talk to you.

JULIE: And I needed some fucking space!

MADDIE: *(Looks at Amy)* Can we have like one minute alone? Please? Just this once.

AMY: I have to pee anyway.

(Amy exits, despite Julie's non-verbal protestations)

JULIE: We're alone. So talk.

MADDIE: How many ways am I supposed to tell you that I'm sorry?

JULIE: I don't think you are sorry, Maddie.

MADDIE: It wasn't on purpose.

JULIE: I said we could go to my place. You refused. You were adamant that we go to your house. Why?

MADDIE: I don't know! Because I wanted you to see where I lived?

JULIE: And we couldn't go to your bedroom…why?
(Maddie does not answer)
    You used me. You didn't have the balls to come out on your own and you used me to do that.

MADDIE: I didn't mean to.

JULIE: But you did.

MADDIE: I told you that I loved you. Many times now. And you've never said a word.

JULIE: I didn't want to lie and profess love when I'm not sure that love is what I was—

MADDIE: You're seriously gonna tell me that you don't feel what I feel? That we're not meant to be together?

JULIE: Jesus Christ, Maddie. We're not actually Jack and Rose on the fucking Titanic, okay? This is real life.

MADDIE: How dare you trivialize my feelings like that?

JULIE: This is all…illusion. Lust. Using romantic fantasies as an escape from--

MADDIE: Escape?
(Beat)
I hate being morbid like this, but I watched my father die, you know. I watched him run out of air, right in front of me. And it wasn't peaceful or calm or any of that shit. It was terrifying and awful and I was there. I watched it happen. THAT'S real. That's reality. And you know who else was there? My mother. Who was so in love with him, and still is, and locks herself in a room obsessively folding birds out of paper in hopes that she can spare someone else what she went through. And you know what? That's real too. Love and reality are not mutually exclusive. Suffering is not the only thing that is real. If it is, then why bother?

(There is a silence)

JULIE: I think you should go.

MADDIE: You can't even respond to what I just said? Seriously?

JULIE: Just go, please. There's no salvaging this wreck of a night.

MADDIE: Can anything be salvaged?
(Julie has turned away)
I guess not.
(Beat)
No matter what, I love you. I'm not sorry that I love you.

(Julie still won't respond. Maddie goes to Julie and kisses her. Julie kisses her back at first, but then pulls away. Maddie waits for something that does not come. After a moment, Maddie exits. Julie sits down on a bar stool. Amy walks back up.)

AMY: You all right?

JULIE: I have no idea.

AMY: Go after her?

JULIE: Why? So we can break up again in two weeks?

AMY: Because you're in love with her?

JULIE: I am intensely infatuated with her.

AMY: You're so in love with that girl you can't see straight.

JULIE: She needs to grow up a little before we can--

84

AMY: Grow up? Look at us. Are we grown ups? I don't
    know.

(Beat)

   I suggest you go and find your pretty young girlfriend
   before she tells you to fuck off and finds someone
   else.

(Lights down)

Scene 5

(Maddie is staring at David asleep on the couch. Maddie is a bit startled, yet curious. Suddenly, she drops her bag on the floor with a thud. David starts awake, sees her.)

DAVID: What?
(David sees Maddie, rubs his eyes, forehead. He focuses)
'Morning.

MADDIE: Well hi there.

DAVID: You must be Maddie.

MADDIE: And you are?

DAVID: I'm a friend of your mother's—

MADDIE: Mona doesn't have any friends.
(David doesn't respond)
So are you guys like....? No. Never mind. That's not possible.

DAVID: What's not possible?

MADDIE: You. My mother. Sexual relations.

DAVID: I had a bad night and your mom let me crash here. That's all.
(Beat. The hangover hits him.)
Ugh. Jesus…

MADDIE: That bottle of vodka has been in the cabinet since like the nineties.

DAVID: Vintage.

MADDIE: You made short work of it.

DAVID: I feel every drop.

MADDIE: Mama only drinks wine these days. Lots of it. But only wine.

DAVID: Your mom was worried about you.

MADDIE: Yes. I can see how wide awake she is, waiting for me.

DAVID: Look, I'm not in any position to say anything—

MADDIE: You're right. You're not in any position.

DAVID: Right. Okay. Sorry.

MADDIE: Where do you know my mother from anyway?

DAVID: We're in the same grief recovery group.

MADDIE: Oh? And what are *you* grieving?

DAVID: Nothing you want to know about.

MADDIE: Oh, come on. What was it? Your grandma die or something?

DAVID: I don't really think you—

MADDIE: Your dog? Goldfish?

DAVID: Actually, my girlfriend was raped and murdered about three years ago. She was on her way home from a night out and a guy followed her to her car. Does that qualify?

MADDIE: Fuck.
(There is a heavy silence)
Jesus. I'm sorry? I hate it when people say that to me.

DAVID: Me too. But what else is there to say?

MADDIE: The world is shit.
(Beat)
So you know all about my dad then?

DAVID: Yes. I'm sorry for that too. From all your mom has told me, it seems like he was a great guy.

MADDIE: The best.
(Beat)
Hey, so I'm not actually a bitch. I just had a really shitty night.

DAVID: There are a lot of shitty nights, aren't there?

MADDIE: Yes. Too many.

(They smile at each other – a truce. Mona pads in, bathrobe, barefoot. Maddie and David both look at her. A slow spread of relief passes over her, but she does not show it.)

MONA: I see you've met my daughter.

DAVID: I have.

MONA: *(To Maddie)* No text message? Voicemail? Something? Honestly, Maddie.

MADDIE: That's it?

MONA: What?

MADDIE: That's all you have to say?

MONA: Is there something else I should be saying?

DAVID: I should probably take off.

MONA: I thought we were getting breakfast?

DAVID: Raincheck?
(Mona looks at him, pleading)
    Next week. I promise.

MONA: Wait.

(Mona goes offstage, returns holding David's clothes)

MONA: Fresh out of the dryer.

DAVID: Thank you.
(David kisses Mona on the cheek, tenderly. David addresses Maddie)
    It was nice meeting you, Maddie.

MADDIE: Likewise.

(David exits. Maddie and Mona are alone)

MONA: Where were you?

MADDIE: I went to talk to Julie. It didn't go very well. So then I just sort of drove around. And then I went to a diner. And I sat there and drank coffee and ate some pancakes. And I realized it was the same diner Dad used to take me to when I was little, and I couldn't deal with it, so I left and I wound up sitting outside on the front steps most of the morning.

MONA: Why didn't you come in?

MADDIE: I just couldn't.

MONA: You can always come home, Maddie.

MADDIE: Is this home, anymore? Really? Do you feel like this is home?

MONA: My home is wherever you are.

MADDIE: But I'm not anywhere.
(Beat)
I think I need to go away. For school. For...life. Whatever.

MONA: Oh.

MADDIE: I know why I stayed...but like...those reasons don't apply anymore. And I'm terrified that if I just keep doing nothing I will be nothing.

MONA: You could never be nothing.

MADDIE: Oh, I could. I could be nothing and do nothing. It wouldn't even be hard. People do it all the time.
(Silence)

And I know it's like…a lot of money and everything but I'll apply for financial aid. It's too late to go anywhere this semester anyway so I guess I'll just get a job and save up.

MONA: Hold that thought.

(Mona goes into the crane room. Maddie follows her but remains in the doorway. Mona opens the desk and pulls out an envelope. Mona hands it to Maddie.)

MONA: Your dad made me promise not to give this to you until you needed it. I guess it's now.

(Maddie opens the envelope. There is a key.)

MADDIE: A key? For what?

MONA: There's a safe deposit box at the bank. There's some cash and savings bonds that your dad wanted you to have, and some other stuff. Not even sure what that stuff is.
(Beat)
Your dad got very cryptic before he died, didn't he? All these secrets and arrangements and "don't open this" and locked boxes and drawers. It's like he was trying to trap the rest of his life in jars, like fireflies or cicadas or--

MADDIE: Why didn't you tell me about this?

MONA: You're not the only one I had allegiances to, you know.

MADDIE: *(Beat)* I've been thinking about Chicago.

MONA: Excellent city. Great parks. Museums. Libraries—

MADDIE: It's far.

MONA: As it should be.

MADDIE: Will you be okay? If I go?

MONA: You're the child. I'm the mom. I don't want you to worry about me.
(Beat)
I'm sorry you didn't feel safe enough to tell me the truth.

MADDIE: I haven't felt safe in a long time, but that's not your fault.

(Mona walks over to Maddie and gives her a big hug)

MONA: Oh, my daughter, you're so lucky to be young. All is not lost, I promise.

MADDIE: David seems really nice. I like him a lot.

(Lights down)

Scene 6

(David is in his apartment. There is a knock at the door. David gets up to answer it. It's Amy.)

AMY: Hi.

DAVID: Amy.

(David doesn't invite her in)

AMY: I was just in the neighborhood, and I—

(Beat. This is ridiculous. Amy talks too fast again)

AMY: Ugh. Yeah, okay, so people say that and it's never true. No one is ever in the neighborhood. No one even talks on the phone anymore, never mind just randomly stopping by. Like who DOES that? So, no, in short I was not actually in the neighborhood but I thought that maybe we could—

(David doesn't move)

AMY: I promise I'm not like…stalking you or anything. I just wanted to give this back to you.

(Amy takes the photo out of her purse, hands it to David, who takes it and looks at it. He lets her in.)

AMY: I shouldn't have taken it. It was wrong and I'm sorry.
(Beat)
   So…sometimes it's like…more interesting to not know things. Like you can make them up and sort of imagine and sometimes that's a lot better than what

actually happened. But at the end of the day, I realized that I wanted to know. I needed to know. So I googled you.

DAVID: Ah.

AMY: I kind of wish I hadn't. What happened to her was--
(There aren't words.)
All I can tell you is that I didn't know. I like to think I'm not a completely terrible person.

DAVID: None of this is your fault.

AMY: It doesn't matter whose fault it is.

DAVID: It does matter. And it's mine. I'm so sorry.
(beat)
I just miss her so fucking much. And that missing turned me into someone I hate.

AMY: I forgive you.

DAVID: Amy...There are... crazy people out there who can hurt you. Who WILL hurt you. And if you keep doing what you're doing...what you did with me...

AMY: Don't worry about me. I can take care of myself.
(Beat)
You know, this is the most you've ever talked to me like...ever.

DAVID: I know.

AMY: It's kind of weird.

DAVID: Tell me about it.

AMY: Can I ask you one question?

DAVID: Sure.

AMY: Why did you ask me not to speak?

DAVID: Because you don't sound like her.

(A beat)

AMY: I should probably go.

(Amy goes to leave)

DAVID: Amy?
(Amy stops)
   Are you gonna be all right?

AMY: I'll be fine.
(Beat)
   You take good care of yourself, okay?

(Amy exits. Lights out)

Scene 7

(Lights come up on the cafe, where Maddie is sitting by herself, having a coffee. She is folding a crane. Julie approaches her. Maddie puts it down.)

JULIE: Hi.

MADDIE: Hey.

JULIE: Thanks for meeting me.

MADDIE: I was out anyway.
(Beat)
He wrote me a letter.

JULIE: Who wrote you a letter?

MADDIE: My dad. It was in a safe deposit box along with some money and some of my grandmother's jewelry. I just saw it today.

JULIE: What did it say?

MADDIE: That he loved me, and that he was proud of me. And that he was sorry for leaving me.
(Maddie starts folding again)
I know it wasn't his fault, but it was nice to hear anyway.

JULIE: I'm so sorry for the things I said to you the other night—

MADDIE: Are you?

JULIE: Yes. Because I love you, Maddie, I do.

MADDIE: You love me?

JULIE: You know that I do.

(They kiss)

MADDIE: *(A beat)* I've decided to go away to school. Grown up college.

JULIE: When?

MADDIE: Next spring.

JULIE: I see.

MADDIE: Chicago.

JULIE: Great town. Horrible winters.

MADDIE: I can't stay here.

JULIE: Of course you can't. I know that.

MADDIE: What do we do now?

JULIE: I don't know. Nothing really to do, I suppose.
(Maddie plays with the crane)
    What are you making?

MADDIE: A paper crane. For my dad. I never made him any when he was sick. Mama taught me all the folds, but I couldn't then.

(Maddie sets the bird on the table. Julie picks it up)

JULIE: Who says you're not artistic? Origami and sculpture are pretty similar, you know.

(Beat)

I brought you something.

(Pulls her sketchbook from her purse, shows it to Maddie)

This is the drawing I did of you that night. Seems so long ago now.

MADDIE: My god. It's...well, it's me, isn't it?

JULIE: How I see you, anyway.

MADDIE: It's beautiful. Thank you. I'll keep it forever.

JULIE: You're welcome.

MADDIE: I don't want to have to say goodbye to you.

JULIE: Why would you? I'm not going anywhere.

(Beat)

I'll come visit you in Chicago. We can go to the Art Institute.

MADDIE: Please. Promise.

JULIE: I promise.

(Lights out)

Scene 8

(Lights up on Mona's house. It is morning. Mona enters the crane room. It looks like she is going to sit down and fold, but instead she opens the drawer and takes out the letter. She takes a deep breath, opens it, and begins to read. It does not take long. Mona turns the letter over to see if anything is written on the back of it, and when she doesn't see anything else, she lets out a cry and begins knocking folded cranes off her desk and tearing them down from the ceiling. Defeated and crying, she sits on the floor and begins to unfold some of the cranes. David approaches, knocks on Mona's front door. She does not answer. David knocks again. Still no answer. David walks into her Mona's house, concerned)

DAVID: Mo?
(Beat)
   Mona?

(David realizes where she is, and approaches the crane room gingerly.)

DAVID: Hi.

MONA: Hey.

DAVID: Your door was open.
(Beat)
   What are you doing?

MONA: I am not *doing*, my darling. I am *un*doing.

(David sits down next to Mona on the floor)

DAVID: Are you okay?

MONA: I realized today that I've spent all this time trying to make a sky when really I was making a fucking noose.

DAVID: It's a beautiful room, Mona.

MONA: I woke up this morning, and started getting ready to go out, and I started to feel terribly guilty about it. Like I hadn't any right. So, I came in here, and instead of folding like I usually do, I decided to finally read that stupid letter I've been torturing myself with. The one I keep talking about.

DAVID: What did it say?

MONA: Nothing. Barely anything. Just that he loved me and that he was sorry for leaving me.

DAVID: What were you expecting?

MONA: I was expecting poetry, dammit! I was expecting the deepest exprcssion of his soul, the culmination of every feeling we'd ever had! Not this limp dick, moist hankie NOTHINGNESS.
(Mona tears a bird apart and throws it)
    FUCK HIM. And fuck these god damn birds!

(David reaches for her, wraps his arms around her)

DAVID: Mo, do you know what was the first thing I thought when I woke up this morning?
(Beat)
    I thought, "I'm getting breakfast with Mona today."
(Beat)
    Do you know what it was like for me to wake up and not immediately want to pull the covers back over my head? To have something to look forward to?

MONA: Oh, David, I'm sorry…

DAVID: Don't be sorry. There's nothing to be sorry for. I just wanted you to know that.

MONA: I was looking forward to it, too.

DAVID: Well, good. Because I'm getting pretty hungry.

MONA: Hollandaise sauce.

DAVID: Right.

MONA: I look awful.

DAVID: You look great.
(Beat)
Hey. You should teach me to make one of those things.

MONA: What? The cranes?

DAVID: Yeah.

MONA: Why?

DAVID: It would be nice to make one for Ashley. I can bring it to the cemetery next time I visit.

MONA: I could make her one, too.

DAVID: That would be nice.

MONA: All right. Then I'm done with the birds. I swear. The last bunch goes to the children's hospital and that's it. I'm staying earth bound from here on out.

(Mona stands up and retrieves some paper from the desk. She hands him a piece. Mona holds up her piece and starts showing him)

MONA: It's really very simple.
    First, fold the paper in half this way…
(Mona folds it in half. David follows)
    Now, unfold it.
(David unfolds it)
    Now you turn the paper and fold it in half again…
(David follows)
    Now unfold it…

(Mona continues to show David the steps as the lights fade.)

END OF PLAY

NOTES

NOTES

Made in the USA
Middletown, DE
15 April 2025